W

MAR 2 8 2016

D0597598

Walla Wa.
County Librar.

HEALTHY ME!

My Body Needs REST

by Jenna Lee Gleisner

J
612.8
Gleisner
2015

amicus
high interest

Amicus High Interest is published by Amicus
P.O. Box 1329, Mankato, MN 56002
www.amicuspublishing.us

Copyright © 2015. International copyright
reserved in all countries. No part of this book
may be reproduced in any form without
written permission from the publisher.

Library of Congress Cataloging-in-Publication Data
Gleisner, Jenna Lee, author.
  My body needs rest / by Jenna Lee Gleisner.
     pages cm. -- (Healthy me!)
  Summary: "Introduces the benefits of rest on the human body, how
much rest young bodies need, and what happens when we sleep while
offering tips to get better rest."-- Provided by publisher.
  Audience: Age 6.
  Audience: K to grade 3.
  Includes index.
  ISBN 978-1-60753-588-1 (hardcover) -- ISBN 978-1-60753-688-8 (pdf
ebook)
  1. Sleep--Physiological aspects--Juvenile literature. 2. Sleep--Juvenile
literature. 3. Health--Juvenile literature. I. Title.
  QP425.G54 2014
  612.8'21083--dc23
                          2013046275

Photo Credits: Leonid Ikan/Shutterstock Images, cover; Shutterstock
Images, 2, 12, 15, 22; Ingram Publishing/Thinkstock, 5; Gina Smith/
Shutterstock Images, 6; Monkey Business Images/Shutterstock Images,
8; Serhiy Kobyakov/Shutterstock Images, 11; Red Line Editorial, 17; Jupiter
Images/Thinkstock, 18; Catherine Yeulet/Thinkstock, 21

Produced for Amicus by The Peterson Publishing Company
and Red Line Editorial.

Designer Becky Daum
Printed in the United States of America
Mankato, MN
1-2014
PA10001
10 9 8 7 6 5 4 3 2 1

TABLE OF CONTENTS

SLEEP

Have you ever gone a day without sleep? We all need sleep. It helps us feel rested. We need sleep to stay healthy.

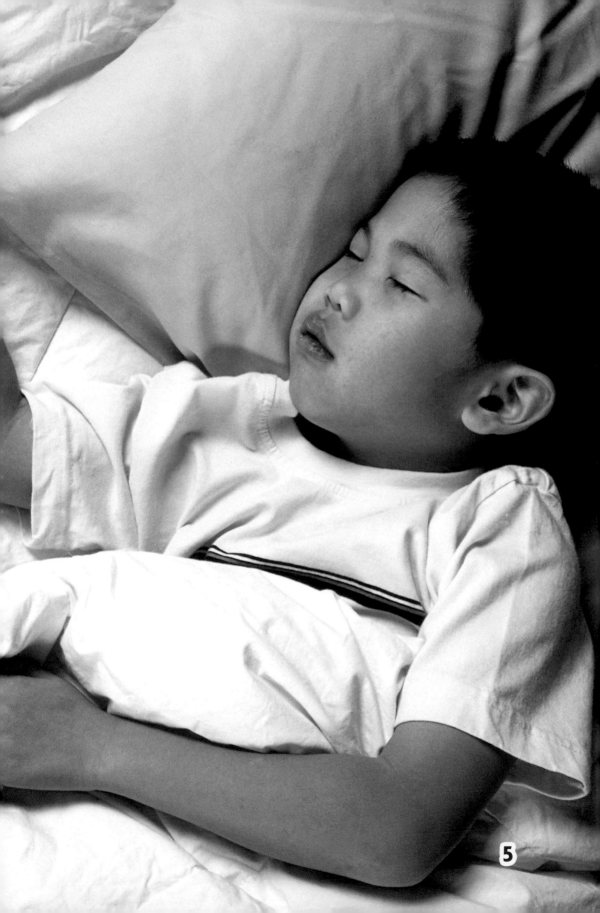

BEDTIME

Young bodies need a lot of sleep. Kids should sleep 10 to 11 hours each night. Set a bedtime. Go to bed at the same time each day.

Healthy Hint

Make your bedroom the best sleeping area. Make it cool, dark, and quiet.

BRAIN POWER

The brain needs sleep. Sleep helps it think and remember. Get enough sleep. This will help you think well in school.

BODY POWER

Sleep also powers the rest of the body. Your **immune system** keeps sickness away. Sleep helps it do its job well. Then your body can fight off a cold or the flu.

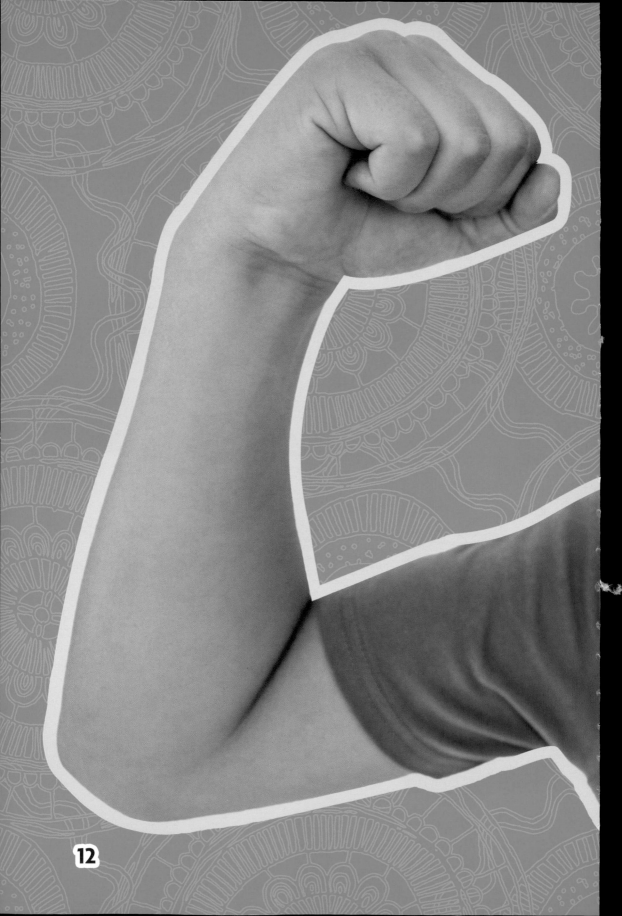

HOW WE GROW

Bones grow the most during sleep. So do muscles. Your brain makes a **growth hormone** when you sleep. The body needs this to grow. Your body does not make enough if you don't sleep enough.

SLEEP STAGES

There are five sleep stages. You start to fall asleep in stage one. Stage two is a light sleep. You are fast asleep by stage three. Stage four is the deepest sleep.

Healthy Hint
Wake up at the same time each day. This will help you sleep better.

SLEEP CYCLE

Rapid eye movement (REM)

sleep is stage five. Your eyes move

quickly. Your brain thinks while you

sleep. People dream in this stage.

You go through all five stages

each night.

STAGE 1
**Drifting Off
to Sleep**
The muscles in your
body relax. You begin
to fall asleep.

STAGE 2
Light Sleep
Your heart starts to
beat slower.

STAGE 3
Deep Sleep
Your brain slows
down.

STAGE 4
Deepest Sleep
It is hard to wake up
from this deep sleep.
Sleepwalking can
happen in this stage.

REM
**Rapid Eye
Movement**
Your eyes move
quickly and your
brain is busy thinking.
Dreaming happens
in this stage.

NEED MORE SLEEP?

Have you ever felt tired? Or crabby? Maybe you did not get enough sleep. This can put you in a bad mood. It can also make you yawn.

Healthy Hint

Turn off TVs and games before bedtime. They give off lights and sounds. These can keep you awake.

RESTED UP

We feel better when we are rested. We can think better at school. We have **energy** to think and play sports. How much sleep do you get each night?

GET STARTED TODAY

- Make your bedroom cool, dark, and quiet for bedtime.

- Wake up and go to bed at the same time each day.

- Turn off TVs, computers, and video games before bedtime.

- Take TVs, computers, and other electronics out of the bedroom.

- Use your bed only for sleeping. Play and do homework somewhere else.

WORDS TO KNOW

energy – power that can be used

growth hormone – a chemical that the body makes to help it grow

immune system – the system that protects the body from sickness and infection

rapid eye movement (REM) – the stage of deep sleep in which the body is completely relaxed while the brain is very active

LEARN MORE

Books

Barraclough, Sue. *Sleep and Rest*. Mankato, MN: Sea-to-Sea Publications, 2012.

Denshire, Jayne. *Rest and Sleep*. Mankato, MN: Smart Apple Media, 2011.

Web Sites
BAM! Body and Mind
http://www.cdc.gov/bam/diseases/immune/immunesys.html
Read more about what makes up the immune system and how it helps fight sickness.

Time for Bed?
http://kidshealth.org/kid/closet/games/bed_game.html
Take a quiz and learn more about why our bodies need sleep!

Why Do I Yawn?
http://kidshealth.org/kid/talk/qa/yawn.html
Learn why you yawn when you are tired.

INDEX